Treasures
We Share

By Della Cohen

Scott Foresman
is an imprint of

Glenview, Illinois • Boston, Massachusetts • Chandler, Arizona •
Upper Saddle River, New Jersey

Photographs

Every effort has been made to secure permission and provide appropriate credit for photographic material. The publisher deeply regrets any omission and pledges to correct errors called to its attention in subsequent editions.

Unless otherwise acknowledged, all photographs are the property of Pearson Education, Inc.

Photo locators denoted as follows: Top (T), Center (C), Bottom (B), Left (L), Right (R), Background (Bkgd)

Opener: Ariel Skelley/CORBIS; **1** ©Britt Erlanson/The Image Bank/Getty Images; **3** ©Radius Images/Jupiter Images; **4** ©Kevin Dodg/Corbis; **5** ©Britt Erlanson/The Image Bank/Getty Images; **6** ©Ariel Skelley/Corbis; **7** ©Radius Images/Jupiter Images; **8** ©Ariel Skelley/Corbis.

ISBN: 13: 978-0-328-46299-5
ISBN 10:   0-328-46299-3

10 V010 14

We share movies.

They are treasures.

We share stories.

They are treasures.

We share pictures.

They are treasures.

We share rocking chairs.
They are treasures.

We share watches.

They are treasures.

We share happy times.
They are treasures too!